Awakening The Light Body: The Shamanic Art Of Alignment And Freedom

Laughing Crow

Published by Laughing Crow, 2025.

AWAKENING THE LIGHT BODY: THE SHAMANIC ART OF ALIGNMENT AND FREEDOM

First edition. March 24, 2025.

Written by Laughing Crow.

Also by Laughing Crow

Awakening The Light Body: The Shamanic Art Of Alignment And
Freedom
Laughing Crow's Teachings - Walking The Sacred Path With Spirit

Watch for more at www.living5d3d.com.

Introduction: The Sacred Dance of Matter, Energy, Emotion, and Permission

In every moment, seen and unseen forces weave the fabric of our reality. We are not merely flesh and bone moving through a linear existence; we are a dynamic interplay of matter, energy, and intention. Like the wind sculpting the dunes, these forces shape our experiences, yet most people remain blind to the depth of their influence.

To walk the shamanic path is to awaken to the great interplay—how the physical body (matter), thoughts (electrical impulses), and emotions (electromagnetic energy) interact to create patterns in our lives. And more importantly, to recognise that within this interplay lies the key to liberation: **permission**—the silent agreements we make with reality.

Eagle Eye, my mentor, once told me, "You are the only one who can open the door, and the only one who keeps it locked." At the time, I nodded, pretending to understand. Years later, through my own struggles and shadow work, his words struck like lightning. The universe does not impose limitations on us—we do that ourselves. We grant permission for what we accept as possible, real, and true. And in doing so, we shape our experience of reality.

This book will serve as an initiation into understanding these forces and, more importantly, how to break free from the illusions that bind you.

The Great Interplay: Matter, Energy, and Emotion in Motion

Our physical form is made of **matter**, an intricate network of molecules held together by unseen forces. Science tells us that at the smallest level, matter is not solid but composed of vibrating particles, pure energy in motion.

Thoughts are electrical impulses firing in the brain, cascading through neural pathways like lightning through a stormy sky. Each thought carries a charge, shaping our perceptions and interactions.

Emotions are more than fleeting feelings; they are electromagnetic fields radiating from our bodies. Science has measured the heart's electromagnetic field as extending several feet beyond us, interacting with everything in its reach. When we experience strong emotions, we shift not only our own energy but the energy of those around us.

Matter, energy, and emotion create an intricate dance. When in harmony, they manifest clarity, vitality, and flow. When in discord, they create stagnation, disease, and limitation.

For example, imagine a person who deeply fears failure. Their thoughts fire off in repetitive, limiting cycles: "I can't," "I shouldn't try," "It won't work." These thoughts generate a biochemical response, releasing stress hormones and tightening the body's muscles (matter). The emotional charge of fear radiates outward, influencing their energetic field. This entire interplay reinforces itself, becoming their reality.

Now, consider someone who shifts their permission—who chooses to believe, "I am capable." Their thoughts change, creating new neural pathways. Their body relaxes, shifting from contraction to openness. Their emotional field resonates differently, attracting new experiences. This shift in permission alters reality itself.

The Power of Permission: Unshackling the Mind

What if I told you that the greatest limits in your life exist because you have given them permission to be there? This is a difficult truth to swallow, but also the most liberating one.

We unconsciously accept boundaries imposed by society, family, past trauma, and personal fears. "I'm not good enough." "I'll never be successful." "I don't deserve love." These are permissions we have granted, whether we realise it or not.

Permission is the doorway between limitation and expansion. When you revoke permission for self-doubt and grant it for possibility, you shift timelines. Your energy changes, your emotions realign, and new realities emerge.

Eagle Eye once challenged me: "When did you decide you couldn't fly?"

I scoffed, thinking he was speaking metaphorically. But he pressed on, "No, truly. When did you accept the idea that the impossible was impossible? Who taught you that?"

That question haunted me. I traced back my limiting beliefs to childhood, to voices of authority, to cultural programming. I realised I had been giving permission for chains that were never mine to wear.

And just like that, I chose to revoke them.

Shamanic Perspective: Awakening the Light Body and Entering Flow

Shamans across cultures understand that reality is not fixed but fluid. Our physical form is but one layer of our being. Beyond it, we have the **Light Body**—an energetic matrix that holds our vitality, intuition, and ability to manifest. When our thoughts, emotions, and matter are in balance, our Light Body activates.

A person in this state radiates presence. They walk into a room, and people feel their energy before they speak. They move through life with synchronicity, meeting the right people at the right time. They heal rapidly, both physically and emotionally. This is not magic; it is alignment.

Flow state—the effortless merging of action and awareness—is a byproduct of aligning these forces. Athletes, musicians, healers, and visionaries tap into this state where time dissolves, and creation happens effortlessly.

To enter flow, you must **allow** it. Release resistance. Give permission to something greater than fear.

An Invitation to Remember

This book is not here to teach you something new—it is here to help you remember what you already know deep within your bones.

The sacred dance of matter, energy, and emotion has always been part of you. The power of permission has always been yours to wield. The wisdom of the ancients whispers through the winds, through the pulse of your heart, through the patterns life places before you.

Will you open the door? Or will you keep it locked?

The choice has always been yours.

The next chapters will take you deeper into the practices, teachings, and experiences that will help you revoke limitations and reclaim your full potential. The path is waiting—step forward.

Chapter 1: Matter – The Body as a Storykeeper

The Storykeeper's Burden – A Teaching from Eagle Eye

Eagle Eye and I sat by the fire one evening, the embers glowing like distant stars fallen to earth. He stared into the flames, silent for a long while, then said, "You ever see a tree try to run away from its roots?"

I shook my head. "No."

He smirked. "Exactly. Because it knows its roots are its strength. But people? People spend their whole lives running from what's inside them—what's written in their bones, their blood, their very breath."

He picked up a small, charred branch and rolled it between his fingers. "Your body is the keeper of all your stories. Every joy, every wound, every unspoken truth—it's all there, waiting to be acknowledged. But instead of listening, most folks ignore the whispers, and when that doesn't work, they numb themselves until the whispers turn to shouts. Pain. Illness. Restlessness. The body will not be silenced forever."

He tossed the branch into the fire and turned to me. "You ever see an old horse carrying too much weight?"

I nodded. "Yeah. It moves slow. Hurts with every step."

"And yet it still tries to keep going," he said. "Until one day, its knees give out. That's what happens when you carry burdens that aren't yours, or when you hold onto grief, anger, or shame that should've been released long ago. The body bends under the weight."

I felt those words settle in my chest, as if my own body recognised their truth before my mind did. "So how do you put the weight down?" I asked.

Eagle Eye smiled. "You listen. You honour what's been carried. You let go of what no longer serves. You stop running from the stories in your bones and start speaking them—through movement, through breath, through ritual. And sometimes..." He leaned closer. "You simply ask your body, 'What are you trying to tell me?' Then, for once, you listen."

He sat back, eyes gleaming like the fire. "Your body remembers what your mind forgets. Will you learn its language?"

The Body as a Living Record

Our bodies are more than just vessels for our consciousness; they are libraries, storing the imprints of our experiences, traumas, and even the echoes of our ancestors. Every scar, ache, and tension carries a story—some we remember, some we have forgotten, and others were written long before we were born.

The tension in your shoulders may not just be from poor posture—it might be the unspoken grief of your grandmother who carried her family through war. The chronic pain in your lower back may not just be a physical ailment—it could be the weight of financial instability passed down from generations. Our bodies are storytellers, whispering truths we may not yet be ready to hear.

In many shamanic traditions, the body is viewed as an extension of the Earth. Just as the land carries the imprints of past civilisations, battles, and ceremonies, our physical form retains the memories of our journey through life. Understanding this opens the doorway to deep healing—when we listen, we can begin to rewrite our story.

The Weight of Suppression: When the Body Speaks Through Illness

Emotions are energy, and energy needs to move. When we suppress emotions—whether grief, anger, fear, or sadness—that energy doesn't disappear. Instead, it finds a home within the body. Over time, unexpressed emotions can manifest as physical symptoms: chronic pain, digestive issues, migraines, or even more severe illnesses.

Modern science has begun to catch up with ancient wisdom, recognising the strong link between emotional trauma and physical health. Studies show that chronic stress and unresolved emotional wounds contribute to inflammation, autoimmune diseases, and cardiovascular issues. But shamans and healers have known this for centuries.

Consider the phrase "a heavy heart." Those who have suffered deep grief often feel a literal weight in their chest, sometimes leading to heart palpitations or breathing difficulties. "Shouldering a burden" isn't just metaphorical—tight shoulders, neck pain, and migraines are common among those who take on the problems of others without addressing their own needs.

In shamanic healing, physical symptoms are seen as messengers rather than enemies. When we stop fighting or numbing the symptoms and start listening to them, we begin the journey of true healing.

Healing Through Awareness: Decoding the Body's Messages

If the body is speaking, the first step toward healing is learning its language. Every discomfort, tension, or recurring illness is a clue to something deeper. Here are a few ways to begin interpreting the messages:

1. **Where is the pain located?** Different parts of the body correlate with different emotional and energetic patterns.
   - Lower back pain? You might be carrying financial fears or a lack of support.
   - Throat issues? Unspoken words, repressed truth, or

fear of expression could be at play.
- ○ Knee pain? Resistance to moving forward or an inability to surrender to life's flow.

2. **What was happening when the symptom appeared?** Illness and pain often surface during times of stress, transition, or emotional upheaval. Did your headaches start when you took on too much responsibility? Did your stomach issues arise when you were suppressing anger?

3. **What emotions are buried beneath?** If you allow yourself to sit with the sensation, what feelings emerge? Fear? Sadness? Rage? Sometimes, the act of acknowledging these emotions is the key to releasing them.

Shamanic Practices for Healing the Body's Stories

Healing is not just about treating symptoms—it's about addressing the root cause. Shamanic traditions offer powerful practices to help us reconnect with our bodies, clear stagnant energy, and release what no longer serves us.

1. Body Listening: A Dialogue with the Self

Find a quiet place where you won't be disturbed. Close your eyes and take a few deep breaths. Bring your awareness to the part of your body that is calling for attention. Place a hand over it if it feels natural. Then, silently or out loud, ask:

- "What do you need to tell me?"
- "What emotion is stored here?"
- "How can I support you in healing?"

Be patient. The answer might come as a word, an image, a feeling, or even a sudden memory. Trust what arises.

2. Grounding Techniques: Releasing Stagnant Energy

Since the body is an extension of the Earth, grounding practices help release stagnant energy. Try walking barefoot on the earth, sitting with your back against a tree, or visualizing roots growing from your feet into the ground, carrying away anything that no longer serves you.

3. Energy Clearing: Removing Residual Trauma

Energy becomes stuck in the body, just as dust accumulates in a house. Smudging with sage, bathing in salt water, or working with sound healing (such as drumming or toning) can help clear out stagnant energy and restore balance.

4. Ancestral Healing: Releasing Inherited Trauma

Since many of our patterns and ailments are inherited, ancestral healing can be a profound practice. Set an intention to connect with your lineage in meditation, asking for guidance on what needs to be healed. Some people find that writing a letter to their ancestors—acknowledging the burdens carried and choosing to release them—brings a deep sense of relief.

Wisdom from One Who Steps Quietly

One Who Steps Quietly, a wise elder in the spirit world, often reminds me that our ancestors are not just those who have passed. They live within us—in our blood, our bones, and our very breath. Healing ourselves is an act of healing them as well.

He once said:

"Your body speaks the language of your ancestors. Will you learn to listen?"

Many of us carry generational wounds without realising it. The fear that grips us, the sadness that lingers, the patterns that repeat—sometimes, these do not even originate with us. But by acknowledging them, we create the space to release them.

Reclaiming the Body's Wisdom

Healing is not about rejecting the body's pain; it is about understanding it. Our bodies are our greatest allies, guiding us toward wholeness with every ache, every tension, and every whisper of discomfort. When we stop ignoring and start listening, we not only heal ourselves but also free future generations from carrying the same burdens.

The journey of healing the body's stories is not about perfection; it is about awareness. The more we listen, the more we uncover, and the more we uncover, the more we step into our true power.

So, what stories is your body telling you today? And are you ready to listen?

Chapter 2: Energy – The Thought Currents That Shape Reality

The Spell You Cast Upon Yourself – A Teaching from Eagle Eye

One afternoon, Eagle Eye had me gather a handful of dry leaves and place them in a circle around us. "Watch," he said, and with a slow breath, he exhaled sharply. The leaves scattered, dancing in the wind.

"Your mind is like that breath," he said. "It stirs the world around you, even when you don't see it."

I nodded, waiting for him to continue. He picked up a single leaf and held it between his fingers. "Every thought you think is a spell. A quiet incantation shaping your reality. Some people wake up every morning and curse themselves without even knowing it."

He mimicked a heavy sigh. "I'm not good enough. I'll never change. Life is hard. No one loves me." Then he tossed the leaf into the wind. "And just like that, the spell is cast. The universe listens, nods, and says, 'As you wish.'"

I shifted uncomfortably. "So what if someone's just... telling the truth?"

Eagle Eye chuckled. "Truth? Or just the same old spell they've been reciting since childhood? If you tell a seed it will never be a tree, and you keep it in the dark, never water it—well, you've made sure it stays just that. But that's not truth. That's neglect."

He pointed at the leaves now scattered far and wide. "The mind does not sit still. It moves, like the wind. If you do not direct it, it will carry your power away, feeding the very things you don't want."

I frowned. "So how do you change the spell?"

Eagle Eye grinned. "Ah. That's the trick most people miss. You stop speaking what you don't want. You speak what you do want. You say, 'I am strong.' You say, 'I am worthy.' You say, 'I am free.' And at first, it will feel like a lie. But a lie repeated long enough becomes truth—just as an old truth, repeated without thought, became your prison."

He stood, brushing off his hands. "Every day, you choose the magic you weave into your world. So tell me..." He looked me square in the eye. "What spell will you cast upon yourself today?"

The Mind as a Conductor of Energy and Belief

The mind is not just a passive observer of reality—it is an active participant in shaping it. Every thought generates an electrical impulse, creating waves of energy that ripple out into the world. These waves influence not only our perception but also the energetic field we move through daily.

Much like a river carves the land over time, our thoughts carve out patterns in our consciousness. The beliefs we reinforce—whether empowering or limiting—become the reality we experience. If you constantly think, "I am not good enough," that thought becomes an energetic blueprint, influencing your emotions, actions, and even how others perceive you. On the other hand, if you affirm, "I am capable and worthy," your energy shifts to align with that reality.

Shamans and mystics have long understood that thoughts are not just fleeting ideas but energetic currents that shape existence. In many traditions, reality is described as a dream, and we, as dreamers, shape it through our intent and focus. If the mind is the conductor, then thoughts are the notes of the symphony we call life.

How Thoughts Become Patterns, and Patterns Become Reality

Every thought carries energy, and when repeated often enough, it creates a pattern. This pattern becomes an ingrained belief, influencing actions and shaping experience. This process is so subtle that we often don't realise it's happening.

Imagine a person who, as a child, was repeatedly told they were not smart. At first, this statement was just someone else's opinion. But as the child internalised it and repeated it in their own mind, it became a belief: "I am not intelligent." Over time, this belief shaped their choices—perhaps they avoided challenging subjects, doubted their ability to learn, or stopped trying altogether. The thought became a self-fulfilling prophecy, creating a reality in which their potential was limited.

Now consider the opposite: a person raised with encouragement, told they are resourceful and intelligent. They are more likely to take risks, explore their abilities, and develop confidence in their capacity to learn. The same world, different thought patterns, vastly different realities.

This is the power of energy in thought. What you focus on expands. The mind directs energy, and energy manifests into form.

The Role of the Subconscious Mind

Most of our thought patterns are not even conscious. The subconscious mind absorbs everything—beliefs from parents, society, media, and past experiences—without questioning their validity. If a limiting belief is embedded deep in the subconscious, it becomes a hidden force shaping reality without our awareness.

This is why deep inner work is necessary. Surface-level affirmations are not enough to rewrite ingrained patterns. We must uncover the root thoughts, question them, and consciously replace them with new ones that support our highest potential.

A simple yet powerful exercise:

- Identify a belief that limits you.
- Ask yourself, "Where did this belief come from? Is it actually true?"
- Imagine letting go of that belief and replacing it with one that empowers you.

Shifting thought patterns is not instantaneous, but with awareness and repetition, you can rewire your mind to generate new energetic currents that align with the life you desire.

Shamanic Perspective: Thoughtforms and the Unseen Energy They Create

Shamanic traditions teach that thoughts are not just intangible concepts but living entities—thoughtforms—that take on a life of their own. A thoughtform is a cluster of energy created by strong mental focus and emotion. If a thought is repeated often enough, it becomes a structured energetic force that can influence reality.

For example, if someone constantly dwells on fear, their thoughtform of fear grows stronger, attracting experiences that reinforce it. This is not superstition—it is the law of resonance. Like attracts like. Negative thoughtforms feed on negative emotions, while positive ones attract opportunities, synchronicities, and expansion.

In shamanic practice, clearing unwanted thoughtforms is a key part of energetic healing. This can be done through rituals, intention-setting, and shifting focus to higher vibrational thoughts.

Practical Ways to Shift Thought Energy

If you recognise that your mind has been shaping a reality that no longer serves you, here are some powerful practices to shift your thought currents:

1. Thought Observation: Becoming Aware of the Inner Dialogue

Spend a day simply noticing your thoughts. Are they self-critical or self-empowering? Are they based on fear or possibility? Awareness is the first step to change.

2. Conscious Reframing: Turning Limiting Beliefs into Empowering Ones

Each time you catch yourself thinking something limiting (e.g., "I can't do this"), immediately replace it with a new thought (e.g., "I am learning and growing"). This rewires the brain over time.

3. Energy Clearing: Removing Old Thoughtforms

- Smudging with sage or palo santo can help dissolve heavy thought energies.
- Sound healing (such as drumming or chanting) can break up stagnant mental patterns.
- Visualisation: Imagine a stream of golden light flowing through your mind, washing away limiting thoughts and replacing them with clarity.

4. Manifestation Through Intentional Thought

- Set a clear intention for what you want to create.

- Focus on it with unwavering belief, as if it is already real.
- Feel the emotion of having it now—emotion is the magnet that amplifies thought energy.
- Release attachment to how it will happen and trust the process.

Wisdom from Pieter: The Power of Thought as Magic

Pieter, a wise guide in the unseen realms, once told me:

"Every belief is a spell you cast upon yourself. Be mindful of your magic."

Just like Eagle Eye, he spoke of thoughts as spells—each one shaping reality in ways we don't always recognise. The question then becomes: Are you casting spells of limitation or spells of liberation?

To reclaim your power, become a conscious spellcaster. Choose your thoughts as deliberately as a shaman chooses sacred herbs for a ceremony. Speak to yourself with reverence. Align your thoughts with your highest truth, and watch as reality reshapes itself around you.

Directing the River of Thought

Your mind is a river of energy, constantly flowing. You can let it carry you mindlessly, shaped by past conditioning, or you can become the shaman of your own consciousness, directing its course with intention and awareness.

Thoughts are not just mental noise—they are currents of creation. With each thought you choose, you shape the world within and around you.

So, what are you creating today?

Chapter 3: Emotion – The Magnetic Force of Creation

What song are you singing to the universe?

I remember a time, long ago, when Eagle Eye took me to a sacred place deep within the hills and creeks of the Australian bush. We had walked for what seemed like hours, winding our way through dense eucalyptus trees, their bark rough and weathered, and crossing over moss-covered rocks beside the clear, flowing creek. The sound of water trickling over stones was a constant companion as we ventured further into the untouched wilderness. Finally, we reached a secluded clearing nestled in the heart of the bush. From the edge of the clearing, we could see the sweeping hills stretching out before us, bathed in the soft light of the late afternoon sun. The air was warm, tinged with the earthy scent of the soil and the sharp freshness of the gum trees. A sense of ancient energy hung in the air, as if the land itself was holding its breath, waiting for something. We sat in silence, listening to the chorus of birds and the whisper of the wind through the branches. It was a place where time seemed to slow, and the spirit of the bush felt alive, resonating with something deeper.

After a long while, Eagle Eye broke the silence. He looked out over the valley, his eyes scanning the horizon. "You see," he said softly, "the land here holds a special energy. It's been this way for eons, shaped by the forces of wind, rain, and fire, but also by the emotions of those who've come before. This place is alive with the energy of those who have loved, feared, laughed, and cried here. All of their emotions have left an imprint."

I nodded, taking in the vastness of the landscape and the silence that enveloped us. But I had more questions than answers.

"Why is that important?" I asked.

Eagle Eye smiled, a knowing glint in his eye. "Because you are not just feeling your emotions. You are broadcasting them. What song are you singing to the universe?"

His words hit me like a wave crashing against the shore. I had always thought of emotions as something I had to endure, manage, or make sense of. But here, in this sacred place, I felt the deep truth of what he was saying: my emotions were not just reactions to the world around me. They were powerful forces in their own right—forces that could shape and shift the world itself. The universe was listening. Every thought, every feeling, every breath, was being received.

Eagle Eye paused for a moment, allowing his words to settle in. Then, as if reading my thoughts, he added, "Every emotion you feel is a frequency. It's a signal you're sending out into the universe. And just like a radio tower, that signal attracts experiences that match the frequency you are emitting."

He looked at me intently. "The question is, what are you attracting?"

At that moment, I realised that the energy I was radiating was directly tied to the life I was living. The fear, the joy, the anger, the love—everything had its own vibrational frequency, and everything I felt was a magnet pulling experiences toward me.

The Heart as a Powerful Electromagnetic Field

If you've ever felt a deep connection to someone just by being near them or experienced a sudden shift in energy when entering a room, you've already felt the electromagnetic power of emotions. What many don't realise is that emotions are not just internal experiences—they are electromagnetic forces that we broadcast outward. The heart, the centre of our emotional body, produces one of the strongest electromagnetic fields in the human body, more powerful than the brain's.

This field doesn't stay contained within us. It extends far beyond the physical body, interacting with the environment and people around us. Just like the radio tower I mentioned, we're constantly broadcasting signals of our emotional state into the world. And just like tuning into a specific station, the frequency of our emotions attracts experiences, people, and situations that resonate with that frequency.

The universe doesn't question your emotional state; it simply mirrors it back to you. The energy you emit is the frequency that the universe responds to. So, when you feel angry, anxious, or frustrated, you are broadcasting a signal that attracts experiences which mirror those emotions. Conversely, when you feel gratitude, love, and joy, you send out a frequency that draws in experiences of abundance, peace, and connection.

Emotions Amplify Manifestations—or Block Them

One of the most profound ways emotions shape our reality is by amplifying—or blocking—manifestations. We all have dreams and desires, whether it's financial abundance, fulfilling relationships, or personal growth. But the emotional energy behind those desires plays a pivotal role in how they manifest.

If you set an intention but are filled with doubt or fear about it, those emotions send out a conflicting signal. While your thoughts may say, "I want this," your emotions are saying, "I'm not sure I deserve this" or "I don't believe this can happen." The universe responds to the emotional frequency, not just the mental one. So, if your heart is not in alignment with your desires, the universe will reflect back the lack of alignment.

Think of it like planting a seed. The thought is the seed, and your emotions are the water and sunlight. If you water the seed with doubt and fear, it struggles to grow. But if you nourish it with love, belief, and excitement, it flourishes.

Shamanic Practices: Emotional Release, Heart Expansion, and Frequency Alignment

Shamanism teaches us to recognise that emotions are powerful tools. They are not just reactions to the outside world but are an integral part of our energetic makeup. To harness the magnetic power of emotions, we must learn how to clear blockages, release negative energy, and align ourselves with the highest vibrations of love, joy, and abundance.

1. Emotional Release

In shamanic traditions, we understand that trapped emotions can create blockages in our energy field, which prevents us from manifesting our desires. Emotional release is a sacred practice of letting go of negative emotions that no longer serve us, allowing our energy to flow freely.

A simple practice to release emotional energy is through breathwork. By breathing deeply into your belly, you connect with the stored emotions within your body. As you exhale, visualise the negative emotions leaving your body as dark smoke, dissipating into the air. This helps to clear the emotional blockages, opening up space for new, more positive energies.

2. Heart Expansion

The heart is the centre of emotional energy, and by expanding the energy of the heart, we expand our capacity to receive and create. Heart expansion is a powerful shamanic practice that helps open us to love, compassion, and gratitude—frequencies that align us with abundance and manifestation.

To practice heart expansion, sit in a quiet space, place your hands over your chest, and focus on your breath. Imagine a warm, golden light growing in your heart center. With each breath, allow that light to expand, filling your entire chest and then radiating outward, touching everything around you. As you breathe in, feel the love and gratitude flowing into your heart. As you exhale, send this energy out into the world, knowing that you are sending out a powerful frequency of abundance and love.

3. Frequency Alignment

To fully harness the power of emotion in manifesting our desires, we must align our energy with the frequency of what we want to create. Shamanic journeying is one way to check in with your emotional state and align yourself with your highest potential.

In a journeying session, ask your spirit guides to help you identify any emotional blockages or misalignments. Ask them to show you what needs to be healed so you can fully align your energy with your desires. When you return from the journey, take note of any insights or messages you received. These insights can serve as reminders to stay aligned with the frequency of your highest good.

You are a creator. What song will you sing today?

It was a cool autumn day when Eagle Eye led me to a hidden valley, a place few had ever visited. The path was narrow and winding, and we had to be careful not to slip on the moss-covered rocks. As we arrived at the valley, Eagle Eye spoke softly, his voice carrying the weight of ancient knowledge.

"This place is sacred," he said. "Not because of its beauty, but because of the emotions it holds. Those who have come here in joy have left that joy behind, and those who have come in pain have left their sorrow. The land itself absorbs and amplifies everything. But the key is this: the energy of this place is not separate from you. It is the energy you carry within you."

I sat down, letting his words sink in. The landscape before me seemed to pulse with life, alive with the imprints of those who had walked this path before me. It was as if the land itself was holding a mirror up to my own emotional state. The trees swayed with the breeze, their leaves shimmering in the light.

Eagle Eye continued, "You have the power to change the energy of any place, any situation, simply by changing your emotional frequency. You are not a passive observer in this world. You are a creator. What song will you sing today? A song of fear and doubt, or a song of love and abundance?"

I looked out at the valley, feeling the energy shift within me. The universe, I realized, was always listening. And it would respond to whatever song I chose to sing.

Your emotions are not just feelings—they are powerful, magnetic forces that shape your reality. The frequency you emit through your emotions attracts experiences, people, and situations that match that vibration. So, ask yourself: What song are you singing today? Is it a song of joy, love, and abundance? Or is it a song of fear, doubt, and limitation?

By practising emotional release, expanding your heart, and aligning with the frequency of your highest desires, you can transform your emotional energy and, in turn, transform your life. The universe is always listening, and it's time to start singing the song of your dreams.

Chapter 4: The Hidden Power of Permission

You create ripples with every thought, every decision, every belief

It was a crisp morning when Eagle Eye led me to a quiet pond deep within the bush. The air was thick with the smell of eucalyptus, and the soft murmur of a distant stream was the only sound breaking the silence. We sat by the water, watching the ripples as they danced across the surface, creating patterns of movement that disappeared as quickly as they appeared.

After a while, Eagle Eye turned to me with a knowing look in his eyes, his voice calm but firm. "Do you see the water?" he asked. "It is still, until something disturbs it. Then, the ripples form, spreading outward. But they cannot go beyond the edge of the pond unless the water allows them."

I nodded, unsure where he was going with this, but trusting that there was something deeper to understand.

"Just like the water," he continued, "your life is shaped by what you allow. You create ripples with every thought, every decision, every belief. But you are the one who sets the boundaries. You will never move beyond what you allow yourself to believe."

The simplicity of his words struck me deeply. My life, my experiences, were like the ripples on that pond, and the scope of those ripples was determined by the invisible contracts and permissions I had given myself.

The Subconscious Contracts We Make with Ourselves

Most of us walk through life unaware of the subtle agreements we've made with ourselves. These agreements—or spiritual contracts—are often formed in moments of emotional intensity, trauma, or simply through repeated thoughts and beliefs. In these moments, we unknowingly decide what is possible for us, what we are worthy of, and what we are allowed to have in life.

These subconscious contracts shape our perceptions and experiences. For example, if you've experienced betrayal in a relationship, you may form an internal contract that says, *"I will never trust fully again."* If you've struggled with financial hardship, you might decide, *"I am not good with money."* These contracts are like invisible fences, keeping us within self-imposed boundaries.

What's dangerous is that we often don't realize we've made these contracts, and therefore, we don't question them. They become a part of who we think we are, influencing our decisions, our relationships, and our ability to grow. The stories we tell ourselves about who we are and what we are capable of come from these hidden contracts. And until we examine them, we remain locked in their confines.

How Permission Shapes Perception and Possibility

Permission is a powerful, yet often overlooked force in our lives. It's the unspoken agreement we make with ourselves about what we are allowed to experience, create, and become. Just as the water cannot flow beyond the pond's edge without permission, we cannot move beyond our own self-imposed limitations without giving ourselves permission to do so.

Think of permission as the key to unlocking your potential. It's the point at which you decide that something is possible for you. It's the moment you give yourself the right to succeed, to love, to grow. Without that permission, your efforts will be half-hearted at best. You might try to push the boundaries, but without a deep, internal acknowledgement that you are worthy of something greater, those efforts will fizzle out.

Permission is not something external; it's something that comes from within. The reality is, you've been conditioned to seek external validation, to look for someone or something else to tell you that it's okay to move forward. But real permission starts with you. It's the moment you decide, *"I am worthy of my dreams. I am allowed to create the life I want. I give myself permission to step into the next chapter of my journey."*

Without this internal permission, you may be stuck in cycles of procrastination, fear, and self-doubt. It's the inner belief that you are not worthy, or that something outside yourself must first change before you can move forward, that keeps you stagnant. True freedom comes from within—and it starts with the simple yet profound act of giving yourself permission.

Shamanic Perspective: Breaking Spiritual Contracts and Rewriting Soul Agreements

From a shamanic perspective, the concept of spiritual contracts and permission is a sacred part of our journey. Shamans understand that the energetic agreements we make, consciously or unconsciously, shape not only our individual lives but also our relationship with the larger universe.

When we enter this world, we often come in with soul agreements—contracts made before this lifetime, either with ourselves or with other beings. These agreements can shape our experiences, the lessons we are meant to learn, and the path we are destined to walk. But as we grow and evolve, it's important to recognise that we have the power to break these contracts and rewrite them, much like we can change the terms of a business deal.

Shamanic practices often involve rituals and journeys designed to uncover these spiritual contracts. Once we become aware of the agreements we've made, we can consciously decide whether they still serve us. If they don't, we can perform rituals to break them, releasing their hold on us. We can then rewrite the soul contracts in alignment with our highest good, creating new agreements that open us up to greater possibilities and more expansive growth.

In shamanic journeying, one can ask their spirit guides to reveal any limiting contracts they've made, whether it's a contract around love, abundance, health, or success. With the guidance of the spirits, you can break free from those contracts and rewrite new ones—ones that allow you to step into your fullest potential.

Believe in your own worth, the universe will reflect that back to you

Eagle Eye and I had just finished a long shamanic drumming journey to a sacred mountain where we had gathered wisdom from the ancient spirits. We sat by a fire, the flames crackling in the stillness of the night, as the stars above seemed to pulse with the energy of the universe.

"You've learned much on this journey," Eagle Eye said, his voice low and measured. "But now you must ask yourself: What is it that holds you back from fully stepping into your power? What invisible contracts are you still bound by?"

I thought long and hard about his question. I had spent years working on my spiritual practices, but there were still areas of my life where I felt stuck. There were dreams I hadn't yet pursued, fears I hadn't yet conquered.

Eagle Eye looked at me with a knowing smile, as though he could see the unspoken thoughts swirling in my mind. "You must give yourself permission to break free," he said. "Give yourself permission to claim the life you desire, without hesitation, without fear of judgement."

He leaned in closer, his eyes intense. "You see, Laughing Crow, the universe is like a mirror. It only reflects what you allow it to. If you remain bound by fear, by past hurts, or by limiting beliefs, that is all you will see. But when you give yourself permission to believe in your own power, to believe in your own worth, the universe will reflect that back to you."

In that moment, something inside me shifted. I realised that I had been holding onto old contracts—contracts of fear, limitation, and unworthiness. It was time to rewrite them, to break free from the chains I had unknowingly placed on myself.

With the clarity of his words, I sat in silence, feeling the weight of those old contracts dissolve. I had given myself permission to step into my fullest potential. And in that permission, I found a freedom I had longed for.

The power of permission cannot be underestimated. The contracts we make with ourselves—often without conscious awareness—limit our potential and shape our reality. But just as we have the power to make those contracts, we also have the power to break them. True freedom comes from within, from the moment we give ourselves permission to grow, to change, and to step into the fullness of who we are meant to be.

By recognising and rewriting our subconscious agreements, we free ourselves to create the life we truly desire. The universe is waiting for you to give yourself permission. The question is, will you?

Chapter 5: Unconscious Permission Slips – Where Did They Come From?

You don't need to carry what was never yours. Set it down.

Eagle Eye and I sat around a crackling fire, its flames dancing and flickering, casting shadows that seemed to shift with the rhythm of the flames. The warmth from the fire wrapped around us, and the night air was cool but not uncomfortable. We sat in silence for a while, listening to the crackle of the fire and the night sounds of the forest.

Finally, Eagle Eye broke the silence, his voice steady and calm, though his gaze was focused on the flames.

"There is something you need to understand before you can move forward. You are carrying things that aren't even yours."

His words hung in the air, and the fire seemed to burn a little brighter in response. I looked at him, but his eyes never left the flames. The weight of his words settled over me like the smoke rising from the fire—lingering, hard to shake off.

I looked at him, confusion clouding my mind. "What do you mean?" I asked.

Eagle Eye's gaze turned toward me, his eyes full of knowing. "You carry the burdens of your ancestors, of your family, and of society. They are not yours to bear, but you've inherited them. Like a blanket wrapped tightly around your shoulders, they weigh you down without you even realising it. And you walk through life, thinking these burdens are yours, but they were placed upon you by the silent agreements you made with the world around you."

I sat quietly, the weight of his words sinking in. He continued, his voice soft but insistent.

"You don't need to carry what was never yours. Set it down."

The simplicity of his words stirred something deep inside me. In that moment, I understood that I had unknowingly accepted unconscious permission slips—agreements that had been handed down from generations past, from society, from family, from trauma. These invisible boundaries had shaped my life, my choices, and my sense of self. But they were not mine to carry. And it was time to let them go.

How Societal, Familial, and Ancestral Conditioning Create Invisible Boundaries

From the moment we are born, we are immersed in a web of invisible conditioning. Our families, societies, and cultures all contribute to the shaping of our beliefs, values, and expectations. These external forces weave stories into our minds, stories that we unconsciously adopt as truth. Over time, we internalize these stories until they become part of who we are, determining the boundaries of what we believe is possible.

Societal conditioning plays a significant role in this process. From an early age, we are taught how to behave, what to aspire to, and what is considered acceptable. These unwritten rules often come with subtle permission slips: *"You are allowed to succeed, but only if you fit into this mould."* Or *"You can dream, but only within the confines of what is socially acceptable."* These agreements are passed down through generations, often without question. We are expected to fit into predefined roles—whether it's the hardworking provider, the dutiful caregiver, or the obedient child—often ignoring the deeper truth of who we are.

Familial conditioning is similarly powerful. The unspoken rules of the family, passed down through generations, form part of the framework within which we operate. If a family has always struggled with money, for example, you might find yourself unconsciously adopting the belief that financial abundance is beyond your reach. If a family has experienced trauma, the belief that safety is something to be feared may become ingrained. These familial beliefs and behaviours are often so deeply rooted that we accept them as part of our identity, unaware that they are the result of silent agreements made long before we were born.

Ancestral conditioning also plays a pivotal role. Many of us carry the wounds of our ancestors—experiences of war, colonisation, displacement, and survival. These traumas become encoded in our DNA, passed down from one generation to the next. We inherit not only the wisdom of our ancestors but also their fears, their unspoken beliefs, and their unresolved pain. These ancestral permissions become part of our internal landscape, shaping how we view the world and our place in it.

The Silent Agreements We Make with Trauma, Unworthiness, and Fear

Much of the unconscious permission we give ourselves comes in the form of silent agreements made with our trauma, unworthiness, and fear. These agreements often arise from deeply painful experiences, shaping our perception of the world and the boundaries we place around ourselves.

When trauma strikes—whether it's a loss, betrayal, or a moment of deep hurt—we often form unconscious agreements with ourselves. These agreements, formed in the heat of emotional pain, may sound something like, *"I will never trust anyone again."* Or *"I am not safe in the world."* These agreements are the mind's way of coping with the overwhelming emotions that trauma brings. They create protective walls, limiting our ability to fully experience life.

Similarly, feelings of unworthiness often arise from these silent agreements. Perhaps you were told, as a child, that you were not good enough or that your dreams were too big. Maybe you were raised in an environment where love was conditional, dependent on meeting certain standards. These early experiences lead to unconscious beliefs that you are not worthy of success, love, or abundance. And you carry those beliefs with you, sometimes without realising they are there, shaping your actions and choices.

Fear, too, creates invisible boundaries. It's natural to fear the unknown, to fear failure, or to fear rejection. But when we allow fear to make decisions for us, we limit ourselves in profound ways. Fear can keep us trapped in situations, relationships, and habits that no longer serve us, simply because we've given it the power to dictate our choices. We unconsciously agree to stay small, to remain safe, and to avoid taking risks that might lead to growth.

These silent agreements often go unchallenged, yet they hold us in place, preventing us from fully stepping into our power and potential. The key to breaking free from these unconscious permissions lies in recognising them for what they are: beliefs and agreements that no longer serve us.

Shamanic Practices: Recognising and Revoking Outdated Permissions

In shamanic practice, one of the first steps in personal growth is to recognise the agreements that are no longer in alignment with our highest good. Just as a gardener must pull weeds to allow the plants to grow, we must consciously examine the beliefs, values, and permissions we've inherited or adopted. These outdated agreements no longer serve us and must be released so that we can grow into the fullest expression of ourselves.

One of the most powerful shamanic practices for this is journeying. Through shamanic journeying, you can enter altered states of consciousness to uncover the hidden agreements that have shaped your life. These journeys allow you to connect with your spirit guides, ancestors, and the land itself, asking them to reveal the invisible contracts you've unknowingly made. Once these contracts are identified, the next step is to revoke them, releasing their hold on you.

Another important practice is to perform ceremonies of release. These can take many forms—from writing down the agreements you want to let go of and burning the paper, to creating a symbolic ritual that represents releasing the weight of inherited beliefs. In these ceremonies, you consciously revoke the permissions you've unconsciously accepted, freeing yourself from the past and stepping into the fullness of your potential.

Let the old pressures wash away, and step into your true self.

Eagle Eye and I were walking along a quiet creek when he paused and pointed to a large rock beside the water. The rock was covered in moss, and the water lapped gently at its base. He looked at me and said, "This rock has been here for centuries. The water has worn away its surface, smoothing it over time. But what you don't see is the pressure beneath the surface. The rock, in its stillness, has allowed the water to shape it. And just like this rock, you've allowed the pressures of the world—society, family, and trauma—to shape you. But it is time to let go of what no longer serves you."

I looked at the rock, suddenly realising how many layers I had built up over the years—layers of beliefs, fears, and conditioning. Like the moss-covered rock, I had allowed the weight of the past to shape me. But it was time to let go.

Eagle Eye smiled gently. "You are not that rock," he said. "You are the water, constantly flowing, constantly changing. You can choose what you allow to shape you. Let the old pressures wash away, and step into your true self."

The unconscious permission slips we carry shape every aspect of our lives—our beliefs, our choices, and our potential. They are often the result of societal, familial, and ancestral conditioning, and they are reinforced by silent agreements made with trauma, fear, and unworthiness. The key to reclaiming our power is recognising these invisible boundaries and consciously revoking them. By doing so, we free ourselves from the past and step into a future where we are no longer bound by outdated permissions.

Through shamanic practices and inner work, we can break the silent agreements that hold us back, allowing us to embrace our true potential and move forward with clarity, purpose, and freedom. It is time to set down the burdens that were never ours to carry and to walk with a lighter heart, unburdened by the past.

Chapter 6: Giving Yourself Permission to Expand

All you need to do is give yourself permission

I remember one of the most powerful lessons I ever received from Eagle Eye. We were sitting by a fire one evening, the sky above dotted with stars, each one seemingly holding a story of its own. The flames flickered, casting soft shadows on our faces, and the air smelled of the earth—earthy, raw, and alive.

Eagle Eye's gaze was steady, his voice as calm and clear as the night air around us.

"The universe does not deny you. Only you do that," he said, his words cutting through the silence like the crackling of the fire. "You are the only one who can limit yourself. You are the only one who can say, 'I am not enough' or 'I am not worthy.' But remember this—those beliefs are not truths. They are permissions you've granted yourself to stay small."

I sat in stillness, his words sinking deep into me. It was as if the fire itself had illuminated the dark places in my heart where self-doubt had lived. Eagle Eye continued, his voice softer now, almost as though he was speaking to the fire itself.

"You have the power to expand beyond what you have allowed yourself to believe. All you need to do is give yourself permission."

How to Consciously Grant Yourself Permission to Heal, Grow, and Evolve

For most of us, growth isn't something that happens by accident. It's something we actively choose. We often wait for external validation or for the universe to give us a sign, believing that permission comes from somewhere or someone else. But in reality, the most important permission you can receive is the one you give yourself.

Granting yourself permission to heal, grow, and evolve is an act of self-love and deep trust. It's an acknowledgement that you deserve to be whole, that you deserve to step into your full power and potential. The key is recognising the places where you have unconsciously placed limits on your own growth and then taking the necessary steps to dissolve those boundaries.

The first step is to become aware of the stories you've been telling yourself. These stories may sound like, *"I'm not ready yet," "I don't have the skills,"* or *"I'm not worthy of success or love."* These are permissions you've unconsciously granted yourself to remain stuck in the same place. To move forward, you must first recognise these self-imposed limitations and decide to rewrite them.

The second step is to create space for expansion. This might mean letting go of old relationships that no longer serve you, releasing limiting beliefs, or allowing yourself to step into new roles. The act of giving yourself permission requires you to release the tight grip you've had on what you thought was possible. It means trusting that you have the capacity to expand and grow beyond the limits of your past.

The third step is practicing patience and compassion with yourself. Giving yourself permission to heal is not about rushing the process. It's about honouring where you are, acknowledging your journey, and allowing yourself the grace to take the steps you need, no matter how small they may seem. Healing and growth are gradual, and sometimes it's about taking one conscious step at a time.

Shifting Self-Limiting Beliefs into Expansive Truths

One of the biggest obstacles to personal growth is the presence of self-limiting beliefs. These are the beliefs that keep us small, that tell us we can't have what we want or achieve what we dream of. But self-limiting beliefs are not inherent truths—they are simply stories we've been telling ourselves for so long that they've become ingrained in our subconscious mind.

To shift these beliefs, we must first become aware of them. Take a moment to reflect on the beliefs you hold about yourself and the world around you. Do you believe you are not worthy of success? Do you believe that growth is difficult or painful? Do you believe you must struggle to be worthy of love? These beliefs are like invisible walls that keep you from expanding.

Once you've identified these limiting beliefs, the next step is to consciously challenge them. Ask yourself questions like, *"Is this belief really true?"* or *"Who told me this? Where did this belief come from?"* Often, self-limiting beliefs are not our own. They are inherited from family, society, or past experiences. When we begin to question these beliefs, we start to see how they no longer serve us.

The next step is to consciously rewrite these beliefs into expansive truths. This process involves transforming the limiting belief into a new statement that aligns with your highest potential. For example, if your limiting belief is, *"I am not worthy of success,"* rewrite it as, *"I am worthy of all the success I desire, and I am open to receiving it."* If you've held the belief that *"healing is hard,"* rewrite it as, *"Healing is a natural process, and I allow myself to heal with ease."*

When you begin to replace your self-limiting beliefs with expansive truths, you open up space for growth and transformation. These new beliefs serve as permission slips that allow you to step into your highest self.

Shamanic Perspective: Calling Back Lost Soul Fragments and Reclaiming Power

In shamanic traditions, we believe that parts of our soul can become lost during traumatic events or periods of emotional upheaval. These soul fragments may be scattered throughout time and space, waiting to be called back into our being. When we experience trauma, whether physical, emotional, or spiritual, we often disconnect from parts of ourselves as a protective mechanism. Over time, these lost fragments can leave us feeling incomplete or fragmented, and our personal power is diminished.

One of the most powerful shamanic practices for expansion is the calling back of these lost soul fragments. This process involves journeying into the spiritual realms to reclaim the parts of ourselves that were left behind in times of pain or fear. By calling these soul fragments back into our being, we reclaim our full power, energy, and potential.

This practice involves deep self-reflection and conscious intention. It requires you to open yourself to the possibility of healing and transformation. When you call back these lost fragments, you allow yourself to integrate the full spectrum of your being—your light and your shadow, your strength and your vulnerability, your past and your present. By reclaiming your soul fragments, you give yourself permission to become whole once again.

The pieces of you that have been lost along the way are still with you, waiting for you to remember.

One day, Eagle Eye and I were walking along the edge of a river. The sun was beginning to set, casting golden light on the rippling water. As we walked, Eagle Eye spoke quietly.

"Sometimes, we lose pieces of ourselves," he said, his voice thoughtful. "We leave them behind in the places we've been hurt or broken. It is as if our soul knows how to protect us by pulling away these parts, keeping them safe. But in doing so, we often forget they're missing."

He paused and looked at me. "The first step in your growth is to call back those lost fragments. You have to give yourself permission to heal fully, to become whole again."

He pointed to the river. "This river is always flowing, always moving forward. It does not stop to look back at the stones it passes. But it never forgets them. It carries the memory of each stone, each turn, each twist. You are like that river—your journey is moving forward, but the pieces of you that have been lost along the way are still with you, waiting for you to remember."

In that moment, I understood. The power to expand, to grow, to heal, had always been mine. I just needed to grant myself permission to reclaim what was lost, to step into the fullness of who I was, and to trust that the universe would always support me in my journey.

Giving yourself permission to expand is not a one-time event—it is an ongoing practice. It requires self-awareness, self-love, and the courage to rewrite the stories that no longer serve you. By consciously granting yourself permission to heal, grow, and evolve, you create space for your highest potential to unfold. Through the practice of calling back lost soul fragments and shifting self-limiting beliefs, you reclaim your power and step into a future that is as expansive as the universe itself.

The universe does not deny you—only you can do that. So, take a deep breath, open your heart, and give yourself permission to become the person you were always meant to be. The journey is yours to claim.

Chapter 7: The Box You Live In – The Power and Danger of Labels

Who are you without the titles, the roles, the masks you wear?

I remember one night when Eagle Eye and I sat together under a vast canopy of stars. We were far from the bustling world, deep within the heart of the Australian bush. The air was heavy with the scent of earth and eucalyptus, and the fire crackled between us, its flames dancing like the spirits of ancestors.

Eagle Eye had been quiet for a long time, his eyes reflecting the firelight, his face serene but thoughtful. Then, without warning, he turned to me, his voice as calm and steady as the earth beneath us.

"Do you know," he began, "that we often carry the weight of labels we did not choose? Some of these labels are given to us, others we pick up along the way, like stones in our pockets. We wear them so long that we forget they are not part of our true self."

I nodded, unsure where he was going with this. He continued, his gaze focused on the stars above.

"These labels can become prisons," he said, "and like prisoners, we begin to believe we are confined to them. But who were you before you decided who you were? Who are you without the titles, the roles, the masks you wear?"

The fire crackled as I sat with his words, letting them sink into me like water into dry soil. In that moment, I realised how many times I had let the labels define me—how many times I had boxed myself into a narrow identity that I thought I had to maintain. The idea of shedding these identities felt both freeing and terrifying at once.

The Power and Danger of Labels

In the modern world, we are conditioned to define ourselves through labels—our job titles, our relationships, our roles in society. We are constantly asked, "Who are you?" And in response, we often give a quick answer, one that reflects the identities we've adopted over the years: *"I am a mother, a healer, a writer, a teacher."*

While these labels can serve a practical purpose, providing structure and clarity in a world that craves definition, they can also become prisons that limit our potential. We begin to associate who we are with these labels, forgetting that they are simply fleeting aspects of our being, not the full truth of who we are.

The danger lies in becoming too attached to these identities. Labels can create a false sense of security, a shield that prevents us from stepping into the unknown. The ego thrives on certainty, and it clings to labels as a way of feeling grounded. But in doing so, we often limit ourselves to a narrow vision of who we could be.

Consider the example of a person who identifies strongly with their role as a "caregiver." Over time, this label may come to define their entire existence. They may neglect their own needs, submerge their desires, and ignore their personal growth in the name of caring for others. While caregiving is a beautiful and necessary role, when it becomes their sole identity, it can trap them in a cycle of self-sacrifice and unfulfilled potential.

Labels can also be dangerous because they often become self-fulfilling prophecies. The moment we decide that we are *something*, we unconsciously start living into that identity. If we define ourselves as *shy*, for example, we may subconsciously act in ways that confirm this belief, avoiding situations that might challenge our perceived identity. In essence, the label becomes a limitation, creating a box we feel obligated to stay inside.

The Ego's Attachment to Limitations Disguised as Certainty

The ego's primary function is to create a sense of identity, to help us navigate the world with a clear sense of who we are. It does this by attaching itself to labels—by giving us a name, a title, a place in the world. This attachment provides comfort because it gives us a sense of certainty. Certainty feels safe to the ego, and so it clings to these labels for dear life.

But here's the thing: the ego's attachment to these limitations is a double-edged sword. While it may offer a sense of security in the short term, it ultimately confines us to a rigid identity that can stifle growth. The ego becomes so focused on preserving the image of who we think we are that it becomes fearful of change.

For example, think of someone who has always been the "funny one" in their social group. Over time, they might feel pressure to maintain that identity, to always be the one cracking jokes or lightening the mood. They may avoid expressing any vulnerability or seriousness for fear of breaking the label they've attached to themselves. The problem with this is that it denies the full spectrum of who they are— their deeper, more complex emotions and desires. The ego, in this case, clings to the label of *"funny one"* at the expense of authentic self-expression.

In this way, labels can trick us into thinking we are the *one thing* they represent, when in truth, we are infinitely more than any single identity.

Shamanic Perspective: Shedding Skins, Dissolving Masks, and Stepping into Fluidity

In shamanic traditions, one of the core practices is the shedding of old skins. This can be understood as the process of releasing the labels, roles, and identities that no longer serve us. The act of shedding is not a rejection of who we have been, but rather a natural evolution—a necessary release in order to step into the fullness of who we are becoming.

The shedding of skins is a metaphor for the dissolution of the masks we wear to protect ourselves from the world. These masks may have been necessary at one point in our lives, but they can become stifling as we grow. When we wear the same mask for too long, it becomes difficult to breathe, to move, to express our true essence.

In shamanic journeying, we often go through rites of passage where we let go of outdated identities—whether that's the identity of the *victim*, the *warrior*, the *rescuer*, or the *saviour*. These roles may have served us once, but they become limiting when they define us for too long. The practice is to embrace fluidity, to allow ourselves to evolve and shift in response to the ever-changing rhythms of life.

Just like a snake sheds its skin to make room for new growth, we too must shed the layers that no longer serve us. This might mean letting go of a career identity that has defined us for decades or releasing a family role that has kept us stuck in a particular way of being. By dissolving these labels, we open ourselves to a life that is not defined by fixed roles but rather by fluid potential.

The Process of Reclaiming Fluidity and Expansion

The first step toward reclaiming fluidity is self-awareness. Begin by examining the roles and identities you hold most dear. Which labels do you carry that no longer serve you? Which ones have become a prison? Are there labels you've adopted out of fear or obligation?

Once you've identified these limiting labels, the next step is to consciously release them. This may require forgiveness—of yourself and others who may have imposed these identities upon you. It may require stepping out of the comfort zone that these labels have created.

To aid in this process, shamanic practices like soul retrieval and journeying can help you reconnect with the parts of yourself that have been hidden beneath these masks. By calling back these lost fragments, you give yourself permission to expand beyond the boundaries of your former self. You embrace the fullness of who you are, both light and shadow, and allow yourself to evolve in a way that is aligned with your truest essence.

A Short Story from Eagle Eye:

One day, while we were walking through scrub, Eagle Eye turned to me and said, "Do you know how much energy you waste trying to hold onto labels?"

I looked at him, puzzled, and he smiled. "When you hold onto a label too tightly, you stop flowing. You stop evolving. You become like a river dammed by a boulder. The water may still move, but it becomes stagnant and trapped."

He paused, watching the sunlight filter through the trees. "You don't need a label to define you. Who you are is like the wind—it moves, it shifts, it flows. To limit yourself is to deny the very essence of life itself."

The labels we wear can either serve us or imprison us, depending on how we relate to them. By shedding the masks we've been conditioned to wear and embracing fluidity, we create the space to evolve and grow in ways we never thought possible.

The universe does not require you to fit into any box. It simply asks you to be, to flow, to expand. You are not your labels, your roles, or your past. You are a vast, ever-changing being, capable of infinite transformation.

So ask yourself: Who were you before you decided who you were? And who could you become if you let go of the box you've been living in?

Chapter 8: Soul Agreements – Contracts That Bind and Free You

Wisdom from Eagle Eye

I remember the night Eagle Eye and I sat by the fire, deep in the bush, where the trees stood like ancient sentinels and the stars watched in silent witness. The embers glowed between us, painting his weathered face with flickers of gold and shadow.

He had been quiet for some time, stirring the fire with a stick, lost in thought. Then, without looking up, he said, "Have you ever noticed how a promise can outlive the one who made it?"

I frowned. "What do you mean?"

He tossed a small twig into the flames, watching it curl into ash. "Long ago, a man once came to me, weighed down by something he couldn't name. He was a good man, hardworking, but no matter how much he tried to move forward in life, something always pulled him back. Opportunities would slip through his fingers. He would start things but never finish. He felt as if an unseen force held him in place."

Eagle Eye finally turned to me, his sharp gaze locking onto mine. "We journeyed together, back through his spirit's path, beyond this life, beyond the stories he had been told. And do you know what we found?"

I shook my head.

"In another lifetime, he had taken a vow—a sacred one. He had been a monk, dedicating himself to a life of silence, humility, and poverty. He had promised never to seek wealth, never to claim power, never to step beyond the walls of his service."

Eagle Eye paused, letting his words settle. "That vow had followed him across lifetimes. It still shaped his path, though he had long forgotten it. His soul still honoured an agreement that no longer served him."

I sat in stunned silence. "So what did you do?"

Eagle Eye smiled. "I asked him a simple question. 'Does this vow still serve you?'"

He let the question hang in the air before continuing. "When he realised it didn't, we helped him release it—unravelling the threads of that old promise, thanking it, and letting it go. From that moment on, his path changed. He was no longer bound to an agreement that had expired long ago."

He poked at the fire again. "Many of us are living under contracts we don't remember signing. Some were made in past lives, others passed down through bloodlines. The question is—do they still serve you?"

How Past-Life and Ancestral Agreements Influence This Life

Not all contracts are written on paper. Some are etched into the soul, whispered across lifetimes, or inherited through ancestral lines. These agreements, often made with the best of intentions, can shape our beliefs, behaviours, and even the circumstances of our lives.

A soul agreement is a binding energetic contract—a promise made at some point in our soul's journey. These agreements can be personal, ancestral, or karmic, and they often dictate the experiences we attract.

Some agreements empower us:

- The healer who has agreed to serve others, lifetime after lifetime.

- The warrior soul who has vowed to protect and uphold truth.
- The seeker who has promised to walk the path of wisdom.

But some agreements, like the one Eagle Eye spoke of, can become outdated, limiting, or even harmful over time. They may have once been blessings but now function as bindings, restricting growth and holding us in cycles that no longer serve our evolution.

Examples of outdated soul contracts:

- A vow of poverty from a past life that keeps you struggling with money.
- An ancestral contract of suffering that perpetuates patterns of trauma in your lineage.
- A past-life promise of servitude that manifests as an inability to set boundaries in relationships.

Without realising it, we may still be honouring agreements that no longer align with who we are today.

Releasing Outdated Soul Contracts That No Longer Serve

Releasing a soul contract does not mean rejecting or dishonouring it. Every agreement was made for a reason. Even the ones that now feel like burdens once held wisdom and purpose. The key is to consciously review these contracts and decide if they still align with your path.

Signs That You May Be Held by an Old Soul Agreement

- Feeling stuck in repetitive patterns despite your best efforts.
- A deep-rooted fear or resistance that doesn't seem to come from this life.
- Unexplained guilt, obligation, or limitation in certain areas of

your life.

- A sense that you are "meant" to suffer, struggle, or serve in ways that deplete you.

Once you recognise the presence of an outdated contract, you have the power to dissolve or rewrite it.

Shamanic Practices: Ceremony for Dissolving and Rewriting Soul Agreements

In shamanic traditions, ceremony is a sacred way to communicate with the spirit world. A soul agreement is an energetic bond, and just as it was created with intention, it must be released with intention.

Step 1: Identifying the Contract

- Sit in stillness and ask, "What agreements am I still honouring that no longer serve me?"
- Pay attention to what arises—memories, emotions, or sudden insights.
- You may receive images, words, or a deep inner knowing.

Step 2: Calling the Agreement Forth

- Light a candle and place a piece of paper in front of you.
- Write down any agreements that come to mind, even if you don't fully understand them.
- Acknowledge the purpose they once served.

Step 3: Honouring and Releasing

- Speak aloud: "I honour this agreement and the wisdom it carried. I thank it for its service. But I am no longer bound by it."

- Burn the paper in the flame, allowing the energy of the contract to be transmuted.
- As the smoke rises, visualise yourself being freed, unbound, stepping into a new way of being.

Step 4: Rewriting a New Agreement

- If the old contract left a void, create a new one that empowers you.
- For example: "I release all vows of poverty and step into abundant flow."
- Or: "I dissolve all contracts of self-sacrifice and reclaim my power."
- Write this new agreement down, speak it aloud, and place it somewhere sacred.

As One Who Steps Quietly says, "Some bindings were once blessings. Make sure they still serve you."

Not all contracts need to be broken—some may still be guiding you in the right direction. But it is up to you to discern which ones are keeping you from your full potential.

The soul is meant to evolve, to expand beyond the limitations of old stories. By consciously choosing which agreements to honour and which to release, you step into a life of greater freedom, alignment, and purpose.

You are not bound by the past unless you choose to be. So, what will you set yourself free from today?

Chapter 9: The Dance of Growth – Embracing Change Without Fear

You are not losing yourself. You are losing who you no longer need to be

I remember the evening Eagle Eye and I sat by the river, the sun melting into the horizon as the water whispered against the rocks. It had been a long day, and my mind was tangled with questions—mostly about the future, about whether I was ready for the changes I felt coming.

Eagle Eye, as always, seemed to know what I was thinking before I spoke. He picked up a small stick and tossed it into the river. We watched it bob and swirl before vanishing downstream.

"The river does not ask permission to keep flowing," he said. "Neither should you."

I frowned. "But what if I'm not ready?"

Eagle Eye chuckled. "Ah, so you think the river waits until it's ready to move forward? Do you think it stops to ask the rocks if it should keep going? No, it flows. It changes. It carves out new paths, and sometimes it floods, sometimes it slows, but it never stops moving. You, too, are a river. You were never meant to stay the same."

I stared at the water, letting his words sink in. "But what if I lose myself in the process?"

He shook his head. "You are not losing yourself. You are losing who you no longer need to be."

Why Spiritual Evolution Requires Shedding Old Versions of Self

We often fear change because we mistake comfort for safety. The mind clings to what it knows, even if what it knows is pain, stagnation, or limitation. But growth—true, deep, soul-level growth—requires that we shed the old skins we've outgrown.

This shedding happens in cycles, just like nature's seasons. Trees do not mourn the loss of their leaves in autumn, nor does a snake weep for the skin it leaves behind. Yet, as humans, we resist. We hold on to identities, beliefs, and patterns that no longer fit us because they are familiar.

Ask yourself:

- What parts of myself have I outgrown?
- What am I holding onto that is holding me back?
- Who would I be if I allowed myself to evolve?

The answers may be uncomfortable, but discomfort is often the first sign of transformation knocking at your door.

Learning to Flow with Transformation Instead of Resisting It

Change is not the enemy. Resistance is.

Think of the times in your life when you have been pushed into change—relationships ending, jobs shifting, paths diverging. How often did those moments, which felt like endings, actually lead to something greater?

Growth does not come in neat, predictable steps. It often comes as:

- Sudden realisations that shake your foundation.

- Life pulling you in an unexpected direction.
- Feeling lost before you find a new version of yourself.

The ego fights change because it wants control, but the soul thrives on expansion. The key is learning to trust the flow rather than fight it.

How to Dance with Change Instead of Resisting It

1. **Recognise When a Cycle is Ending**
   - Pay attention to feelings of restlessness, frustration, or disconnection.
   - These are signs that an old version of you is ready to fall away.
2. **Let Go of the Need to Know What's Next**
   - Growth is not a straight path; it is a spiral.
   - Trust that each step will reveal itself when the time is right.
3. **Surrender to the Process**
   - Stop gripping onto what no longer serves you.
   - Allow yourself to release old identities and step into the unknown.
4. **Honour the Death and Rebirth Cycle**
   - Every major transformation involves a symbolic death—the end of an old self.
   - Instead of fearing it, honour it as an initiation into something greater.

Shamanic Perspective: The Initiation of Death and Rebirth Cycles

In shamanic traditions, transformation is not seen as a single event but as an ongoing cycle of death and rebirth. This is why initiation rites often involve symbolic death—because to step into a new version of yourself, the old version must dissolve.

The *death* in these cycles is not physical but spiritual:

- The death of limiting beliefs.
- The death of old identities.
- The death of attachments that no longer serve.

This is followed by *rebirth*:

- A deeper connection to your true self.
- Expanded awareness and new ways of being.
- A greater alignment with your purpose.

Many people resist these cycles because they fear the unknown. But what if, instead of fearing change, you welcomed it as an ally? What if you trusted that every death was simply making way for a new beginning?

Eagle Eye's words echo in my mind often: "You are not losing yourself. You are losing who you no longer need to be."

The river does not resist its journey. It does not fight the rocks or try to flow backward. It moves forward, reshaping itself along the way.

And so must we.

Growth is not about becoming someone new. It is about remembering who you were before fear, conditioning, and limitation told you otherwise.

So the question is—will you cling to the shore, or will you let yourself flow?

Chapter 10: The Light Body – What It Means to Be Fully Aligned

The Essence of the Light Body

In shamanic wisdom, the Light Body is not something you attain—it is something you uncover. It is the luminous essence that has always been there, buried beneath layers of conditioning, fear, and limitation. Many traditions speak of this concept differently: in Andean shamanism, it is the *poq'po*—the energy field surrounding and permeating the physical form. In some Indigenous traditions, it is the *spirit body*, the aspect of self that remains untethered by time or limitation. In the simplest terms, stepping into your Light Body is stepping into your full power, free of the distortions that have kept you small.

Pieter says, ***"You do not need to seek your light. You need only remove what dims it."*** This is the heart of the journey. The Light Body is not something you build—it is something you remember, something you embody as you shed the burdens that do not belong to you.

The Integration of Body, Mind, and Heart

To awaken the Light Body is to bring these three aspects of self into alignment:

- **The Body:** A sacred vessel, a bridge between the seen and unseen worlds. It carries ancestral wisdom, past experiences, and the imprints of all that has come before.
- **The Mind:** A powerful conductor of energy. Thoughts shape reality, creating structures that either illuminate the path or obscure it.
- **The Heart:** The electromagnetic center of creation. It is the seat of emotion, the portal to intuition, and the force that

binds the spirit to purpose.

When these three elements move in harmony, the Light Body activates. Energy flows freely, intuition sharpens, and life becomes a dance of synchronicity.

Signs You Are Moving Into Alignment

Stepping into your Light Body is not a single moment of enlightenment—it is a process of gradual illumination. Some signs that you are moving into alignment include:

- Increased intuition and a stronger connection to inner knowing.
- A sense of deep peace, even in the midst of challenges.
- Physical vitality and a release of chronic pain or tension.
- Heightened awareness of energy, synchronicities, and the unseen world.
- A natural shedding of relationships, habits, or beliefs that no longer serve you.

Shamanic Practices for Activating and Strengthening the Light Body

1. Energy Clearing and Releasing Density

The Light Body cannot shine when weighed down by stagnant energy. Use practices such as:

- Fire ceremonies to transmute old energy.
- Smudging with sage, palo santo, or cedar to clear the field.
- Breathwork and movement to release stored tension in the body.

2. Sun and Earth Connection

The Light Body responds to both solar and earthly energies. Daily connection with the sun strengthens the luminous field, while grounding with the earth ensures stability. Walk barefoot, sit with your back against a tree, or place your hands on the soil to anchor your energy.

3. Dreamwork and Journeying

The Light Body operates beyond time and space. In shamanic journeying and dreamwork, you can access deeper aspects of your luminous self, reclaim lost power, and receive guidance on your path.

4. Heart Expansion and Coherence

The heart emits the most powerful electromagnetic field in the body. Practices such as gratitude, breathwork, and meditations on love and compassion strengthen its resonance, allowing the Light Body to fully activate.

Wisdom Story from Eagle Eye: "The Boy Who Carried Stones"

Eagle Eye once told me a story of a young boy who wanted to become a great warrior. He sought the wisdom of an elder, who gave him a heavy sack of stones and told him to carry it everywhere he went. The boy did so, believing that the weight would make him stronger.

Years passed, and the boy became a man, still carrying his sack. His back ached, his steps were slow, but he refused to set it down. One day, the elder returned and asked, "Why do you still carry that?"

"Because you told me to," the man replied.

The elder smiled. "I told you to carry it to understand its weight. Not to make it your burden."

The man opened the sack and looked at the stones. Each one had a word carved into it: Fear. Doubt. Regret. Guilt. He had been carrying his past, his wounds, and his fears—believing they made him strong, when in truth, they had only made him heavy.

"True power is not in carrying the weight," the elder said. "It is in knowing when to set it down."

That day, the man placed the stones upon the ground and walked away lighter. For the first time in his life, he felt his own lightness—his own Light Body shining through.

Stepping into Your Power

In shamanic terms, the awakening of the Light Body is stepping fully into your power. This does not mean overpowering others, nor does it mean seeking external validation. It means standing in the truth of who you are—unburdened, unafraid, and aligned with your highest self.

The more you release what is not yours, the more your Light Body shines. The more you align with your heart's truth, the more your reality shifts. The more you embrace the path of integration, the more your luminous self emerges.

Eagle Eye's wisdom lingers: ***"True power is not in carrying the weight. It is in knowing when to set it down."***

So, I ask you—what stones are you ready to lay down?

Chapter 11: Living in Alignment – Practical Habits for Lasting Transformation

Shamanic practice is not something you do, it is something you are

One evening, as the fire crackled and the stars stretched across the sky like an ancient tapestry, I sat across from Eagle Eye, feeling frustrated.

"I don't understand," I said, stirring the embers with a stick. "I meditate, I drum, I journey—but only on the weekends. During the week, life takes over, and I feel disconnected. It's like I have to start all over every time. How do I stay in the flow?"

Eagle Eye chuckled, tossing a handful of herbs into the flames. The smoke curled upward like a serpent dancing toward the moon.

"Let me tell you a story," he said. "There was once a man who wanted to learn the way of the hunter. He trained on Sundays. He practiced drawing his bow, moving silently through the forest, tracking footprints in the dirt. But on Monday, he went back to his village life—feet heavy, ears deaf to the sounds of the wind, eyes blind to the shifting patterns of nature. When the next Sunday came, he found he had forgotten much. His muscles were stiff, his aim was off, and the animals had long learned to avoid him."

I frowned. "That seems foolish. I would imagine that a real hunter must always be aware, always in practice, or he will never survive in the wild."

Eagle Eye smiled. "Ah, and yet you think the way of the shaman is different? The spirits do not leave you because the weekend is over. The wind does not stop speaking, the fire does not forget its stories, and your soul does not stop listening. It is you who turns away. And so, each time you return, you feel as though you must begin again."

I kept silent, staring into the flames.

"Shamanic practice is not something you do," Eagle Eye continued. "It is something you ***are***. *It is in how you breathe, how you listen, how you walk in this world. Every moment is a ceremony, every interaction a sacred exchange. The spirits do not work on schedules. Either you walk the path, or you don't. The choice is yours."*

The fire popped, sending a spray of sparks into the night. I nodded slowly.

"I understand now," I whispered.

"Good," Eagle Eye said, leaning back. "Then stop trying to fit the sacred into your life. Let your life ***be*** *the sacred."*

The Wisdom of the Old Tracker

There was an old Aboriginal tracker named Wari, known for his ability to navigate the harshest landscapes with an ease that baffled outsiders. One day, a young man asked Wari, "How do you always find your way, even when there are no clear tracks?" Wari smiled and tapped his chest. "The land is not separate from me. I listen. I feel. If I walk with respect, the path always reveals itself. If I rush, if I doubt, if I let fear take me, I lose the way. The path does not disappear; only my ability to see it does."

The young man furrowed his brow. "But what if you are lost? What if you cannot see the path?"

Wari chuckled. "Then I stop. I breathe. I let the land speak to me again. The path is always there. But you must be still enough to see it."

Walking in Alignment

Living in alignment is not about perfection. It is about presence. It is about maintaining a state where body, mind, and heart move in harmony, allowing the Light Body to remain active and clear. It does not mean life will never challenge you, but it does mean you will navigate those challenges with clarity, resilience, and a deep connection to your own wisdom.

Just as Wari trusted the land to reveal the path, we must trust our own being to guide us. The problem arises when we allow fear, doubt, or distraction to cloud our connection to our inner compass. That is why cultivating daily practices to maintain balance is crucial.

Practical Habits for Lasting Transformation

1. Energetic Hygiene

Just as we clean our physical bodies, we must also cleanse our energy fields. Throughout the day, we collect emotions, thoughts, and energies from others that can weigh us down and distort our clarity. Regular energetic cleansing keeps your Light Body strong and fluid.

- **Daily Practice:** Smudging with sage, palo santo, or eucalyptus can clear stagnant energy. Taking salt baths or spending time in natural bodies of water also helps to reset your field.
- **Shamanic Technique:** Visualise a waterfall of light washing over you, dissolving all attachments and restoring your true essence.

2. Mindful Awareness & Thought Discipline

The mind is a powerful tool, but it can also become a prison if we let it run unchecked. When we become conscious of our thoughts, we begin to recognise self-imposed limitations and shift into expansive perspectives.

- **Daily Practice:** Spend a few moments each morning setting an intention for how you want to think and feel throughout the day. If negative thoughts arise, acknowledge them but do not entertain them.
- **Shamanic Perspective:** Words are spells. Be mindful of the language you use about yourself and your life. Speak in a way that reinforces your growth and alignment.

3. Emotional Mastery

Emotions are the magnetic force that shapes reality. When we suppress them, they become stagnant energy in the body. When we express them with awareness, they become fuel for transformation.

- **Daily Practice:** If you feel emotionally overwhelmed, pause. Breathe deeply. Identify the emotion, honour it, and then release it through movement, sound, or writing.
- **Shamanic Perspective:** The drumbeat mimics the heart. Drumming or chanting helps shift emotional energy and bring the heart into coherence.

4. Grounding & Embodiment

To live in alignment, we must stay connected to our bodies. A scattered mind and an ungrounded spirit lead to imbalance and disconnection from intuition.

- **Daily Practice:** Walk barefoot on the earth, touch trees, or simply take deep breaths while focusing on your feet. Eat grounding foods and stay hydrated.
- **Shamanic Technique:** Imagine roots growing from your feet deep into the earth, anchoring you. This stabilizes your energy and keeps you present.

5. Living with Integrity

Integrity is alignment in action. It means your thoughts, words, and actions reflect your truth. When you betray your own values, you create inner discord and weaken your Light Body.

- **Daily Practice:** Before making a decision, ask yourself, "Does this choice align with who I truly am?"
- **Shamanic Perspective:** In indigenous traditions, the path of the warrior is one of honour. Live in such a way that your spirit remains untangled and free.

Navigating Challenges Without Slipping Back

Even with the best intentions, challenges will arise. The key is not to avoid difficulty but to respond to it with awareness and adaptability. Here are some ways to stay aligned even in turbulent times:

- **When doubt creeps in:** Recall a moment when you were deeply connected to your path. Anchor into that knowing.

- **When fear arises:** Instead of resisting fear, acknowledge it and move through it. Fear only controls us when we avoid facing it.
- **When you feel lost:** Just as Wari said, stop. Breathe. The path is not gone; your mind has simply obscured it. Reconnect to your heart and intuition.
- **When old patterns emerge:** Recognise them without judgement. Shift focus to what serves you now, not what once defined you.

Walking the Sacred Path with Awareness and Integrity

There is no "final destination" in spiritual growth. The path is ongoing, always unfolding. The goal is not to reach an endpoint but to walk with presence and trust, knowing that each step shapes the next.

When we integrate these practices into daily life, we no longer live from reaction but from conscious choice. We cultivate resilience, clarity, and deep connection to the greater web of existence.

As One Who Steps Quietly reminds us:

"The path is never straight, but it is always yours to walk."

Are you living in a way that reflects your true essence? If not, what small shift can you make today? The journey of alignment is not about grand gestures; it is about consistent, intentional steps.

The path is before you. Walk it with awareness, and it will always reveal the way.

Conclusion: The Final Permission – Claiming Your Power

The Illusion of Smallness

The journey you have taken through these pages has been one of unlearning, of remembering, of shedding the false skins that bound you to limitation. You have been guided to listen to the whispers of your body, the currents of your mind, and the rhythm of your emotions. You have been shown that permission is not something granted by the world outside you—but by the vastness within you.

Now, as you stand at this threshold, there is only one truth left to embrace: **You were never small. You only believed you were.**

Eagle Eye once told me a story about this very thing:

Wisdom Story: The Caged Eagle

One afternoon, as we sat beneath a towering gum tree, Eagle Eye pointed to the sky where an eagle soared high above us. Its wings stretched wide, gliding effortlessly on the winds.

"Do you see that one?" he asked.

"Yes," I answered, shading my eyes.

He nodded. "Let me tell you a story. Once, there was an eagle that was taken from its nest as a chick and raised among chickens. It scratched at the dirt, pecked at grains, and never lifted its eyes to the sky. It did not know it could fly. It believed it was a chicken because that was what it had always been told."

He glanced at me, waiting. I knew better than to interrupt.

"One day, a strong wind came, and the eagle felt something stir deep inside—a calling, a memory it did not understand. It watched as a wild eagle flew overhead, something about it familiar yet distant. For the first time, the eagle spread its wings. It was clumsy at first, uncertain. The chickens clucked and told it to stop, that it was foolish, that the sky was not for creatures like them."

Eagle Eye smirked. "But the eagle no longer listened. It leapt, caught the wind, and rose higher and higher until it was no longer a chicken pretending to be small—but an eagle remembering what it had always been."

He looked at me then, his dark eyes sharp as flint. "You see? The eagle was never small. It only believed it was. And so do you."

Recognising Yourself as the Creator of Your Experience

For most of your life, you have lived within stories—some inherited, some self-imposed. Stories of unworthiness, of limitation, of doubt. You have been told where your place is, what you can and cannot do, how high you are allowed to soar. But just like the eagle in the story, **those stories were never the truth.**

The truth is this: **You are the creator of your experience.**

Reality does not shape you—you shape it. Your thoughts, your beliefs, your emotions, and your choices weave the world around you. You are not a victim of circumstance, not a passive observer in your own life. You are the dreamer **and** the dream.

So, what will you choose to create?

Will you choose to stay grounded with the chickens, scratching at the surface of life? Or will you give yourself permission to **fly**?

Fully Stepping Into Your Truth

Stepping into your truth means embracing your power without hesitation. It means no longer waiting for permission to be who you were always meant to be. It means recognizing that every limitation you ever faced was only as real as the belief that held it in place.

You are not small. You are not weak. You are not lost.

You **are** limitless.

A Final Invitation

This book has not been a set of teachings—it has been an initiation. You were not simply reading words; you were shifting, breaking, remembering. You were shedding old skins and stepping forward as something more.

Now, there is nothing left to do but to **live** this truth.

Let your voice ring out. Let your presence be felt. Let your spirit shine.

Eagle Eye's words echo one last time:

"You were never small. You only believed you were."

It's time to remember. It's time to fly.

About the Author

Laughing Crow is a shamanic practitioner, storyteller, and mentor who has walked the sacred path for many years, learning from wisdom keepers, elders, and the land itself. With deep roots in both Native American and Indigenous Australian teachings, as well as influences from Eastern and Western spiritual traditions, Laughing Crow brings an expansive, grounded, and often humorous approach to spirituality.

Guided by the wisdom of his elders and mentors, spirit guides like Pieter and One Who Steps Quietly, and his own lived experiences, he shares teachings that bridge the seen and unseen worlds. Whether leading shamanic breathwork journeys, drumming fire circles, or mentoring seekers on their path, his mission is to help others step into their authenticity, deepen their connection with Spirit, and walk the path of balance, presence, and joy.

Laughing Crow shares his wisdom through *Spirit Echoes: Laughing Crow's Teachings*, a podcast and online community dedicated to exploring signs, synchronicities, and the universal energy that guides us all. When not teaching, he enjoys time with his partner, Kerri, and guiding the next generation—including his own children—through the sacred journey of life.

With humour, heart, and a deep reverence for the mysteries of existence, Laughing Crow invites you to listen, laugh, and walk the path with Spirit at your side.

Read more at www.living5d3d.com.

Manufactured by Amazon.ca
Acheson, AB

16512787R00044